ECE KARADAG

Philosophical Investigations

for mom and dad

Contents

1

Absurd and Absurdity

Absurdity is a facet of life that often leaves us baffled, amused, or even frustrated. It's the quality of being wildly irrational, illogical, or incongruous with our expectations or understanding of the world. The concept of absurdity is deeply rooted in existentialist philosophy, particularly popularized by thinkers like Albert Camus and Jean-Paul Sartre in the mid-20th century.

At its core, absurdity challenges our notions of meaning and purpose. It thrusts us into situations where reason fails to provide satisfactory explanations, and where the human condition appears absurdly insignificant in the vast expanse of the universe. Take, for instance, the image of Sisyphus endlessly rolling a boulder up a hill in Greek mythology, only for it to roll back down each time he nears the summit. This futile and repetitive task epitomizes the absurdity of existence – a ceaseless struggle with no ultimate resolution or meaning.

Absurdity often manifests in everyday life through situations that defy logic or common sense. From the nonsensical bureaucracy depicted in Kafka's works to the absurdity of war portrayed in Heller's "Catch-22," we encounter absurdity in various forms. It's evident in the quirks of human behavior, the paradoxes of society, and the absurdities of nature itself.

Yet, despite its seemingly negative connotations, absurdity also holds a certain allure. It prompts us to question the status quo, challenge conventions, and find humor in the absurdity of our own existence. In a world filled with uncertainties and contradictions, embracing the absurd can be a liberating act – a recognition of the absurdity of our predicament and a willingness to laugh in the face of adversity.

In literature, theater, and art, absurdity often serves as a powerful tool for satire and social commentary. Through exaggeration and juxtaposition, artists highlight the absurdities of the human condition and invite audiences to reflect on their own lives and society as a whole.

Ultimately, absurdity reminds us of the inherent irrationality of the world and the limitations of our understanding. It challenges us to find meaning in the midst of chaos and to embrace the absurdity of existence with courage, humor, and resilience. As Camus famously wrote, "The struggle itself towards the heights is enough to fill a man's heart. One must imagine Sisyphus happy."

Indeed, Camus's notion of imagining Sisyphus happy encapsulates a profound acceptance of the absurdity of life. Despite the seemingly futile nature of his task, Sisyphus finds fulfillment in the sheer act of persevering. This perspective invites us to reconsider our own struggles and find meaning not in the outcome, but in the process itself.

In the realm of philosophy, existentialism embraces the absurd as an inherent aspect of human existence. Existentialist thinkers emphasize the individual's freedom to create meaning in a seemingly meaningless world. In confronting the absurd, they argue, we are confronted with the fundamental choice to either despair or rebel against the absurdity and live authentically.

Theater of the absurd, a genre that emerged in the mid-20th century, embodies these existentialist themes through its portrayal of characters trapped in nonsensical situations. Playwrights like Samuel Beckett and Eugene Ionesco depict the absurdity of human existence through surreal dialogue, absurd plots, and minimalist settings. Through their works, they invite audiences to confront the absurdity of their own lives and society.

In contemporary culture, the absurd continues to be a source of fascination and inspiration. From absurdist memes and internet humor to avant-garde art installations, artists explore the absurdity of contemporary life in innovative ways. By embracing the absurd, they challenge societal norms and conventions, inviting audiences to question their own perceptions and beliefs.

Ultimately, the absurd reminds us of the inherent unpredictability and irrationality of the world. It invites us to embrace ambiguity, confront uncertainty, and find meaning in the midst of chaos. Whether through philosophy, literature, or art, the exploration of absurdity offers a profound opportunity for self-reflection and existential inquiry. In a universe devoid of inherent meaning, it is up to each individual to create their own sense of purpose and significance in the face of the absurd.

In the face of absurdity, individuals may grapple with existential questions about the meaning of life, the nature of reality, and their place in the universe. Some may find solace in existentialist philosophy, which advocates for personal responsibility and the pursuit of authenticity in the face of life's absurdities. Others may turn to religion or spirituality in search of transcendental truths that provide comfort and guidance in uncertain times.

Moreover, humor often serves as a coping mechanism in the face of absurdity. Satirical comedians, absurd comedies, and dark humor offer a lens through which to view the absurdities of life with a sense of levity and perspective. By laughing at the absurd, individuals can momentarily transcend the limitations of their circumstances and find solidarity in shared absurd experiences.

However, it's essential to acknowledge that the absurd can also evoke feelings of discomfort, anxiety, and nihilism. Confronting the irrationality of existence may lead some individuals to question the value of their actions and beliefs, or even to spiral into existential despair. In these moments, it's crucial to seek support from loved ones, mental health professionals, or existential counselors who can provide guidance and perspective.

In navigating the absurdities of life, it's essential to cultivate resilience, curiosity, and compassion. Embracing the absurdity of existence doesn't mean resigning oneself to passivity or apathy; rather, it invites individuals to engage with life's uncertainties with courage and open-mindedness. By embracing the absurd, individuals can find liberation from the constraints of societal expectations and discover new possibilities for personal growth and self-discovery.

In conclusion, the concept of absurdity offers a rich tapestry of philosophical inquiry, artistic expression, and existential reflection. Whether encountered in literature, theater, or everyday life, the absurd challenges individuals to confront the inherent contradictions and uncertainties of existence with courage, humor, and resilience. In embracing the absurd, individuals can find liberation from the shackles of conventional wisdom and embark on a journey of self-discovery and existential fulfillment.

2

What is the meaning of life beyond meaning?

Existential crises are like unexpected storms in the vast sea of our lives, tossing us into the turbulent waters of uncertainty and introspection. They often emerge when we confront the fundamental questions of existence: Who am I? What is my purpose? What does it all mean? These questions, though universal, strike at the core of our individuality, challenging our beliefs, values, and perceptions of reality.

During an existential crisis, the ground beneath our feet seems to vanish, leaving us adrift in a boundless void of doubt and anxiety. We may feel disconnected from our surroundings, alienated from others, and estranged from ourselves. It's as if we're standing at the edge of an abyss, peering into the abyss of our own existence, grappling with the enormity of our own insignificance.

Yet, amidst the chaos of existential turmoil, there lies an opportunity for profound growth and self-discovery. Like a phoenix rising from the ashes, we can emerge from the depths of our crisis with a renewed sense of purpose and clarity. By confronting our existential fears head-on, we can strip away the layers of illusion and pretense that obscure our true selves, embracing the raw authenticity of our being.

In the throes of an existential crisis, we may find solace in philosophy, spirituality, art, or simply in the act of connecting with others who share our struggles. These moments of connection serve as beacons of light in the darkness, guiding us towards a deeper understanding of ourselves and our place in the universe.

Ultimately, an existential crisis is not a sign of weakness, but rather a testament to our capacity for introspection and growth. It is a reminder that life is not always neatly packaged or easily understood, but rather a journey fraught with uncertainty and complexity. And in embracing the uncertainty, we can find the freedom to create meaning in our own lives, forging our own path through the existential wilderness.

In navigating the labyrinth of an existential crisis, we often confront the harsh reality of our mortality. The awareness of our finite existence can be both sobering and liberating, prompting us to reevaluate our priorities and seize the fleeting moments of life with newfound fervor.

For some, the existential crisis may manifest as a profound sense of nihilism, a belief that life is ultimately meaningless and devoid of purpose. Yet, even in the face of such nihilistic despair, there is room for resilience and defiance. We can choose to rebel against the absurdity of existence by embracing our autonomy and creating our own meaning in a seemingly indifferent universe.

Others may find themselves grappling with existential anxiety, a persistent fear of the unknown and the existential void that lurks beyond the horizon of our understanding. In these moments of existential dread, it's important to cultivate a sense of acceptance and surrender, acknowledging the inherent uncertainty of life while finding solace in the beauty of the present moment.

Ultimately, the journey through an existential crisis is a deeply personal one, shaped by our unique experiences, beliefs, and perspectives. It is a journey of self-discovery and self-acceptance, a quest to reconcile the contradictions and complexities of our existence.

In the end, an existential crisis is not something to be feared or avoided, but rather embraced as an integral part of the human experience. It is through the crucible of crisis that we are forged into more resilient, compassionate, and authentic versions of ourselves, ever-evolving on the journey towards self-realization and enlightenment.

Delving deeper into the labyrinthine depths of an existential crisis, one encounters the unsettling realization that the constructs upon which we have built our lives are but fragile facades, easily shattered by the weight of existential inquiry. It's as if we are confronted with a mirror reflecting not only our outward appearance but also the fractured fragments of our innermost thoughts and fears.

In the midst of such existential turmoil, the once-familiar contours of reality begin to blur, revealing the underlying chaos and uncertainty that lurks beneath the surface of our everyday lives. The reassuring certainties that once anchored our sense of self are now called into question, leaving us adrift in a sea of existential ambiguity.

At the heart of the existential crisis lies a profound sense of disorientation, a feeling of being untethered from the moorings of identity and purpose. We may find ourselves grappling with the gnawing sense of emptiness that accompanies the recognition of our own mortality, the fleeting nature of our existence laid bare before us like a stark, unyielding truth.

In these moments of existential reckoning, we are forced to confront the fundamental absurdity of the human condition, the inherent contradictions and paradoxes that define our existence. It's as if we are actors on a cosmic stage, performing our roles with a sense of urgency and desperation, knowing full well that the final curtain call is inevitable.

Yet, within the crucible of existential crisis lies the potential for profound transformation and transcendence. It is through the process of confronting our existential fears and embracing the inherent uncertainty of life that we are able to transcend the limitations of our ego-driven selves and tap into a deeper, more expansive dimension of consciousness.

In this space of existential openness and vulnerability, we may catch glimpses of a transcendent truth beyond the confines of our individual selves, a truth that speaks to the interconnectedness of all things and the inherent beauty of existence itself. It is here, amidst the ruins of our existential crisis, that we may find redemption and renewal, emerging from the darkness with a newfound sense of clarity and purpose.

As we continue to navigate the murky waters of existential crisis, we are confronted with the daunting task of reconstructing our shattered sense of self amidst the rubble of disillusionment. It's a process akin to piecing together a mosaic from fragments of broken glass, each shard a reflection of our inner turmoil and existential angst.

In this journey of reconstruction, we are called to delve deep into the recesses of our psyche, confronting the shadowy aspects of our being that we may have long ignored or suppressed.

We must confront our deepest fears, insecurities, and existential doubts with unwavering courage and self-compassion, for it is only by embracing our darkness that we can truly come to know the light.

As we sift through the debris of our existential crisis, we may unearth hidden treasures of wisdom and insight that have lain dormant within us, waiting to be discovered. We may find solace in the teachings of ancient philosophers, mystics, and sages who have grappled with the same existential questions that plague us today. Their words of wisdom serve as guiding stars in the darkness, illuminating the path forward with their timeless truths and profound insights.

In the process of rebuilding ourselves from the ground up, we may discover newfound strengths, talents, and passions that we never knew existed within us. We may forge deeper connections with others who have walked a similar path, finding solace and camaraderie in shared struggles and shared triumphs. And through it all, we may come to realize that our existential crisis was not a curse but a blessing in disguise, a catalyst for growth, transformation, and self-actualization.

In the end, an existential crisis is not a destination but a journey, a journey of self-discovery and self-actualization that leads us ever closer to the truth of who we are and why we are here. It is a journey fraught with challenges and uncertainties, but also with endless possibilities and infinite potential. And as we emerge from the depths of our existential crisis, we do so not as the same person who entered, but as a wiser, stronger, and more authentic version of ourselves, ready to embrace the beauty and complexity of life in all its myriad forms.

As we emerge from the depths of our existential crisis, we do so not as the same person who entered, but as a wiser, stronger, and more authentic version of ourselves, ready to embrace the beauty and complexity of life in all its myriad forms. We carry with us the scars of our struggles as badges of honor, reminders of the resilience and courage that reside within us.

Armed with newfound clarity and purpose, we embark on a journey of self-expression and self-creation, charting a course towards a future imbued with meaning and significance. We may stumble along the way, faltering in the face of adversity and uncertainty, but we press onward, fueled by the unwavering conviction that our lives are a canvas upon which we alone hold the brush.

In the end, it is not the answers we seek that define us, but the questions we dare to ask and the journey we undertake in pursuit of truth and understanding. And though the road ahead may be long and arduous, we take solace in the knowledge that we are not alone, for we are all fellow travelers on the winding path of existence, navigating the twists and turns of our shared humanity with courage, compassion, and grace.

3

What is Philosophy? A Search for Meaning in Meaninglessness?

Philosophy, often regarded as the love of wisdom, is a timeless endeavor that delves into the fundamental questions of existence, knowledge, reality, and ethics. At its core, philosophy is a relentless search for meaning amidst the apparent meaninglessness of the world. It confronts the perplexing aspects of human existence, challenging us to grapple with the ambiguity and uncertainty that surround us.

One of the central pursuits of philosophy is to unravel the mysteries of existence and to make sense of the world in which we find ourselves. It questions the nature of reality, asking whether there are objective truths that transcend our subjective experiences or if reality is merely a construct of our perceptions and interpretations.

In the face of a seemingly chaotic and random universe, philosophy seeks to find patterns, order, and purpose. It explores the nature of causality, chance, and determinism, pondering whether there is inherent meaning or if meaning is something we impose upon the world.

Moreover, philosophy is a discipline that challenges our assumptions and beliefs, encouraging critical thinking and intellectual inquiry. It invites us to question the foundations of our knowledge and to examine the validity of our convictions. Through philosophical inquiry, we confront our biases, prejudices, and preconceptions, striving for a deeper understanding of ourselves and the world around us.

Yet, perhaps paradoxically, philosophy also embraces the ambiguity and uncertainty of human existence. It acknowledges the limits of human reason and the inherent mysteries that may never be fully comprehended. In this sense, philosophy is not merely a quest for definitive answers but an ongoing dialogue, a perpetual journey of discovery and exploration.

Ultimately, philosophy offers a means of navigating the complexities of life and finding meaning in a world that often appears indifferent to our existence. It invites us to engage with the profound questions that lie at the heart of the human experience, inviting us to ponder the meaning of meaninglessness and to find wisdom amidst the uncertainty of existence.

In this pursuit, philosophy serves as a beacon of intellectual inquiry, guiding us through the labyrinth of existence and challenging us to confront the existential dilemmas that define the human condition. It encourages us to contemplate the nature of reality, the essence of truth, the origins of morality, and the significance of our own existence.

Moreover, philosophy provides a framework for grappling with the inherent tensions between freedom and determinism, individuality and community, reason and emotion. It prompts us to examine the ethical implications of our actions and decisions, urging us to strive for a deeper understanding of our responsibilities to ourselves, to others, and to the world at large.

At its core, philosophy is a reflection of the human spirit, a testament to our capacity for curiosity, wonder, and introspection. It is a discipline that transcends cultural boundaries and historical epochs, offering timeless insights into the nature of reality and the human experience.

In essence, philosophy is a search for meaning in meaninglessness, a journey of intellectual exploration that challenges us to confront the uncertainties and ambiguities of existence with courage and curiosity. It invites us to embrace the inherent complexity of life and to find solace in the pursuit of wisdom amidst the vastness of the unknown.

Philosophy invites us to engage with the profound questions that lie at the heart of the human experience, such as: What is the nature of consciousness? Do we possess free will, or are our actions predetermined by external forces? What is the source of moral values, and do they exist independently of human perception?

As we delve deeper into these inquiries, we may find ourselves confronting the limits of human understanding. Philosophy encourages us to acknowledge the vastness of the universe and our limited perspective within it. It challenges us to embrace humility in the face of uncertainty and to recognize that some questions may never have definitive answers.

Yet, despite the inherent challenges, philosophy offers us a means of finding meaning and purpose in our lives. It provides us with a framework for self-reflection and personal growth, enabling us to cultivate virtues such as empathy, compassion, and intellectual humility.

Moreover, philosophy fosters a sense of interconnectedness

with others and with the world around us. By engaging in philosophical dialogue and debate, we can gain new perspectives and insights that enrich our understanding of ourselves and our place in the universe.

In this way, philosophy serves as a beacon of light in the darkness, guiding us through the existential abyss and helping us to find meaning in the midst of meaninglessness. It is a journey of exploration and discovery, a quest for wisdom that enriches our lives and deepens our understanding of the human experience.

In conclusion, philosophy is not merely a search for meaning in meaninglessness; it is an ongoing journey of intellectual exploration, ethical inquiry, and existential reflection. It challenges us to confront the uncertainties of existence with courage and curiosity, inviting us to engage with the profound questions that shape the human experience.

Through philosophy, we come to appreciate the richness and complexity of life, embracing the inherent ambiguity and uncertainty that define our existence. It is a discipline that celebrates the diversity of human thought and experience, encouraging us to seek wisdom and understanding in the face of the unknown.

Ultimately, philosophy offers us a path to transcendence, guiding us towards a deeper understanding of ourselves, the world, and our place within it. It is a testament to the enduring quest for knowledge and wisdom that defines the human spirit, reminding us of the boundless potential of the human mind to illuminate the darkest corners of the universe and find meaning amidst the chaos.

4

Is everything we see a reflection or an illusion?

In the labyrinth of human perception, the question arises: Is everything we see a reflection or an illusion? This inquiry delves into the very nature of reality, challenging our understanding of the world around us and the faculties through which we apprehend it.

At first glance, our perception of reality seems straightforward. We trust in the reliability of our senses, believing that what we see, hear, touch, taste, and smell accurately reflects the world as it exists independently of our consciousness. Yet, upon closer examination, cracks begin to appear in this seemingly solid foundation.

Consider the phenomenon of optical illusions, where our senses deceive us into perceiving something that contradicts objective reality. These perceptual distortions remind us that our senses are not infallible arbiters of truth but rather imperfect filters through which we interpret the external world.

Moreover, advancements in fields such as neuroscience and psychology have revealed the intricate workings of the human mind, highlighting the role of cognitive biases, cultural conditioning, and subconscious influences in shaping our perception of reality. Our brains construct a subjective representation of the world based on a complex interplay of sensory data, memories, emotions, and beliefs, leading to the possibility that what we perceive may be more a reflection of our internal state than an accurate portrayal of external reality.

Furthermore, the advent of technologies like virtual reality and augmented reality further blurs the line between perception and illusion. These immersive experiences demonstrate our capacity to create convincing simulations of reality, prompting us to question the distinction between the genuine and the artificial.

In the realm of philosophy, thinkers from Plato to Descartes have pondered the nature of reality and the possibility of deception. Plato's allegory of the cave illustrates how our perception of reality may be akin to shadows dancing on the walls of a cave, with the true essence of things lying beyond our sensory apprehension. Descartes famously doubted the veracity of his perceptions, positing the existence of an evil demon capable of deceiving him about the nature of reality.

Ultimately, the question of whether everything we see is a reflection or an illusion challenges us to reconsider our assumptions about the nature of reality and the limits of human knowledge. It invites us to cultivate a skeptical mindset, questioning the veracity of our perceptions and remaining open to alternative interpretations of the world.

In the face of uncertainty, we must embrace a stance of epistemic humility, acknowledging the limitations of our understanding while remaining committed to the pursuit of truth. Whether reality is ultimately a reflection of some deeper truth or an elaborate illusion may remain an enigma, but it is through the ongoing dialogue and exploration of such philosophical questions that we inch closer to a deeper understanding of ourselves and the universe in which we dwell.

In navigating the intricate terrain of perception and reality, we encounter profound philosophical inquiries that probe the very essence of existence. One such question pertains to the nature of consciousness itself: are our subjective experiences a faithful reflection of an external reality, or are they, too, a construct of our minds?

Philosophers have long grappled with the concept of subjective experience, pondering the relationship between consciousness and the external world. The idealist tradition, exemplified by thinkers like George Berkeley, posits that reality is fundamentally mental in nature, existing only insofar as it is perceived by a conscious mind. From this perspective, everything we perceive is indeed a reflection, albeit one that originates within the confines of our own consciousness.

Conversely, proponents of realism argue that there exists an objective reality independent of human perception, which exists regardless of whether it is observed or experienced. According to this view, our perceptions may provide imperfect representations of reality, but they nevertheless offer glimpses into an external world that exists beyond the confines of our minds.

Furthermore, the advent of quantum physics has introduced additional layers of complexity to our understanding of reality. Quantum phenomena such as superposition and entanglement challenge our intuitive notions of space, time, and causality, raising the possibility that reality may be far stranger and more elusive than we previously imagined.

In light of these considerations, the distinction between reflection and illusion becomes increasingly blurred. Perhaps reality is neither a faithful reflection nor a mere illusion but rather a multifaceted tapestry woven from the interplay of consciousness and the external world.

Ultimately, the quest to unravel the mysteries of perception and reality invites us to adopt a nuanced perspective that embraces the complexities of human experience. Whether everything we see is a reflection or an illusion may ultimately depend on the framework through which we interpret the world, highlighting the subjective nature of perception and the inherent limitations of human knowledge.

In this ongoing exploration of perception and reality, philosophy serves as a guiding light, illuminating the contours of our understanding and inspiring us to probe ever deeper into the mysteries of existence. As we navigate the labyrinth of consciousness and confront the enigma of reality, we embark on a journey of philosophical inquiry that transcends the boundaries of perception and beckons us towards a deeper understanding of the nature of existence itself.

Furthermore, the exploration of whether everything we see is a reflection or an illusion prompts us to consider the interplay between perception and reality. It challenges us to recognize that our understanding of the world is shaped not only by external stimuli but also by internal processes of interpretation and meaning-making.

In contemplating this question, we confront the possibility that our perception of reality may be inherently subjective, colored by our individual experiences, beliefs, and cultural frameworks. What appears to one person as a reflection of truth may be perceived by another as a mere illusion, highlighting the relativity of human perception.

Moreover, the notion that everything we see is a reflection raises profound metaphysical questions about the nature of existence itself. If reality is indeed a reflection, what then is the source of this reflection? Is there an underlying substrate of ultimate reality beyond the realm of appearances, or are we forever confined to the surface level of phenomena?

Similarly, if everything we see is an illusion, what implications does this have for our understanding of truth and knowledge? Can we ever escape the web of deception that surrounds us, or are we condemned to forever wander in a hall of mirrors, chasing after shadows that vanish upon closer inspection?

While these questions may seem daunting, they also offer an opportunity for philosophical inquiry and introspection. By probing the nature of perception and reality, we gain insights into the human condition and the mysteries of existence. We come to appreciate the complexity and ambiguity of the world, embracing the uncertainty that accompanies our quest for understanding.

In the end, the question of whether everything we see is a reflection or an illusion serves as a reminder of the profound mysteries that lie at the heart of reality. It challenges us to confront our assumptions, question our perceptions, and remain open to the possibility of deeper truths awaiting discovery. And perhaps, in our relentless pursuit of meaning and understanding, we may catch a glimpse of the underlying unity that transcends the dichotomy of reflection and illusion, illuminating the path toward a more profound comprehension of the universe and our place within it.

5

Nothingness in being or nothingness in nothingness?

In the vast expanse of philosophical inquiry, the concept of nothingness occupies a central and enigmatic position. It is a theme that resonates across cultures, epochs, and disciplines, inviting us to confront the profound mysteries of existence and non-existence, being and nothingness.

At its core, the exploration of nothingness encompasses two distinct yet interconnected dimensions: nothingness in being and nothingness in nothingness. Each dimension offers its own unique insights into the nature of reality and the human condition, challenging us to navigate the intricate interplay between existence and absence, presence and absence.

Nothingness in being beckons us to contemplate the inherent emptiness that pervades the fabric of existence. It is a recognition that beneath the surface of apparent solidity and substance lies a fundamental void, a space of potentiality and negation. In this sense, nothingness in being serves as a reminder of the impermanence and transience of all things, urging us to embrace the fleeting nature of existence and to find meaning amidst the ebb and flow of life.

Yet, nothingness in being is not merely a void to be feared or avoided. It is also a source of creative potentiality, a wellspring from which new forms, ideas, and possibilities emerge. In embracing nothingness in being, we open ourselves to the transformative power of emptiness, allowing ourselves to be shaped and molded by the forces of change and renewal.

On the other hand, nothingness in nothingness plunges us into the abyss of pure negation, where even the most basic categories of thought and existence dissolve into nothingness. It is a realm of absolute emptiness, devoid of form, substance, or meaning. In confronting nothingness in nothingness, we encounter the limits of human understanding and the unfathomable depths of the void.

Yet, paradoxically, it is within this abyss of nothingness that we may glimpse the possibility of transcendence and liberation. For in surrendering to nothingness in nothingness, we release ourselves from the constraints of ego, desire, and attachment, opening ourselves to the boundless expanse of the infinite.

In the dialectic between nothingness in being and nothingness in nothingness, we find a profound synthesis of opposites, a reconciliation of presence and absence, existence and non-existence. It is a dynamic interplay that lies at the heart of the human experience, challenging us to confront the existential paradoxes that define our lives.

Ultimately, the exploration of nothingness invites us to embrace the full spectrum of human experience, from the depths of despair to the heights of transcendence. It is a journey of self-discovery and self-transformation, leading us ever closer to the elusive truth that lies beyond the veil of appearances. And in our quest for understanding, we may come to realize that nothingness is not a void to be feared, but a gateway to deeper insights, greater wisdom, and profounder truths.

Nothingness is a concept that has fascinated philosophers and thinkers throughout history, provoking profound questions about the nature of existence and the limits of human understanding. Within philosophical discourse, nothingness can be explored in two distinct yet interconnected contexts: nothingness in being and nothingness in nothingness.

In the context of being, nothingness refers to the absence or lack of something within the framework of existence. This absence can manifest in various forms, such as the absence of physical objects in a space, the absence of meaning or purpose in life, or the absence of inherent value or significance in the universe. Nothingness in being challenges us to confront the limitations of our perception and understanding, prompting us to question the nature of reality and the meaning we ascribe to it.

One of the most prominent philosophical explorations of nothingness in being is found in existential philosophy, particularly in the works of thinkers such as Jean-Paul Sartre and Martin Heidegger. Sartre famously argued that human existence is characterized by a fundamental nothingness, a lack of inherent essence or meaning that confronts us with the responsibility to create our own values and meanings in a world devoid of inherent significance.

Heidegger, on the other hand, explored the concept of nothingness as part of his broader investigation into the nature of being. He argued that nothingness is not simply a void or absence but is rather an integral part of being-in-the-world, shaping our experience and understanding of reality.

In contrast, nothingness in nothingness refers to a more abstract and metaphysical concept of nothingness that transcends the realm of being altogether. This form of nothingness is not simply the absence of something but is rather a state of non-being that exists beyond the confines of existence.

Within this context, nothingness in nothingness challenges us to confront the ultimate limits of human comprehension. It raises questions about the nature of reality itself, asking whether there is a state of absolute nothingness that precedes or transcends existence.

Philosophers such as Hegel and Nietzsche have grappled with the concept of nothingness in nothingness, each offering their own interpretations and insights. Hegel, for instance, viewed nothingness as a necessary component of the dialectical process, arguing that it is through the negation of existing states of being that higher forms of reality emerge.

Nietzsche, on the other hand, rejected the idea of nothingness as a transcendent state, instead embracing a more life-affirming philosophy that celebrated the creative power of human existence in the face of an indifferent universe.

In conclusion, the concept of nothingness in being and nothingness in nothingness challenges us to confront the limitations of our understanding and to explore the nature of reality in all its complexity. Whether viewed as an absence within existence or as a transcendent state beyond being, nothingness serves as a provocative philosophical concept that encourages us to question, reflect, and seek deeper insights into the mysteries of existence.

Within the exploration of nothingness in being and nothingness in nothingness lies a profound invitation to delve into the very essence of existence and non-existence. It prompts us to question not only what is, but also what is not, and to consider the intricate interplay between presence and absence, being and non-being.

In contemplating nothingness in being, we confront the existential void that underlies human existence. This void, far from being a mere absence, serves as a fertile ground for the cultivation of meaning, purpose, and identity. It is within this existential nothingness that we are confronted with the freedom and responsibility to define ourselves and our place in the world.

Moreover, nothingness in being challenges us to reevaluate our preconceptions about reality and the nature of truth. It encourages us to recognize the inherent limitations of our perceptions and understanding, inviting us to embrace the uncertainty and ambiguity that accompany the human experience.

On the other hand, nothingness in nothingness beckons us to confront the ultimate mystery of existence itself. It raises profound metaphysical questions about the nature of reality beyond the confines of empirical observation and rational inquiry. Is there a state of absolute nothingness that precedes or transcends existence? Or does nothingness merely serve as a conceptual placeholder for the limits of human comprehension?

Philosophers and mystics throughout history have offered diverse interpretations of nothingness in nothingness, ranging from the nihilistic void of existential despair to the transcendent emptiness of spiritual enlightenment. Yet, regardless of the particular perspective one adopts, the exploration of nothingness in nothingness invites us to confront the ineffable mystery at the heart of existence and to embrace the inherent uncertainty and unknowability of reality.

In the end, the exploration of nothingness in being and

nothingness in nothingness serves as a profound philosophical inquiry into the nature of existence, consciousness, and reality itself. It challenges us to transcend the confines of our everyday perceptions and to engage in a deeper reflection on the mysteries that lie at the heart of the human experience. And while the answers to these questions may remain elusive, it is in the pursuit of understanding that we find meaning, purpose, and fulfillment in our journey through the enigmatic landscape of existence.

In essence, the exploration of nothingness in being and nothingness in nothingness invites us to embark on a journey of profound philosophical inquiry, probing the depths of existence and non-existence alike. It challenges us to confront the mysteries of reality, the limitations of human understanding, and the fundamental nature of being itself.

Whether viewed as an existential void within the framework of existence or as a transcendent state beyond the confines of being, nothingness beckons us to contemplate the ultimate questions of existence with humility, curiosity, and awe. It reminds us of the inherent limitations of our perceptions and understanding, urging us to approach the mysteries of the universe with an open mind and a spirit of inquiry.

In the face of the vast unknown, we are called upon to embrace the uncertainty and ambiguity that define the human condition. For it is in the exploration of nothingness—in all its manifestations—that we discover new perspectives, insights, and truths that illuminate the path toward a deeper understanding of ourselves and the universe in which we dwell.

6

What is Beyond Thinking?

Beyond thinking lies a realm both mysterious and profound, where the boundaries of logic and rationality dissolve into the ineffable depths of human experience. In this enigmatic domain, language falters, concepts crumble, and the mind relinquishes its hold on comprehension. What lies beyond thinking is not merely the absence of thought but a dimension of existence that transcends the limitations of intellect.

At the heart of this inquiry lies the recognition that human cognition, while a remarkable tool for understanding the world, is inherently limited. Our thoughts are shaped by language, culture, and personal experience, constraining our perception within the confines of familiar paradigms and preconceived notions. Yet, there exists a vast expanse of reality that eludes the grasp of conceptual understanding – a realm of intuition, emotion, and ineffable beauty that defies logical explanation.

Beyond thinking lies the realm of intuition, where insights emerge from the depths of consciousness without the intermediary of conscious reasoning. Intuition transcends the linear progression of thought, offering glimpses into hidden truths and subtle connections that elude rational analysis. It is through intuition that artists create masterpieces, scientists make groundbreaking discoveries, and mystics attain glimpses of the divine.

Furthermore, beyond thinking lies the realm of emotion, where the raw intensity of human experience defies the neat categorization of language and logic. Emotions like love, awe, and existential angst cannot be fully captured or understood through rational analysis alone. They resonate with a primal energy that speaks to the depths of our being, evoking responses that transcend the boundaries of thought.

Moreover, beyond thinking lies the realm of spirituality, where seekers grapple with questions of meaning, purpose, and the nature of existence. Spiritual experiences often defy rational explanation, transcending the limitations of language and intellect to reveal profound truths about the nature of reality and the human condition. Whether through meditation, prayer, or mystical contemplation, individuals seek to connect with something greater than themselves, venturing into the unknown reaches of consciousness in pursuit of transcendence.

In conclusion, what lies beyond thinking is a realm of mystery, wonder, and infinite possibility. It is a domain where the boundaries of intellect are transcended, and the full spectrum of human experience unfolds in all its richness and complexity. While thinking is a valuable tool for understanding the world, it is only by venturing beyond its confines that we can truly apprehend the depths of reality and the fullness of our own existence.

7

What is Consciousness?

Consciousness stands as one of the most profound and enigmatic aspects of human existence, captivating philosophers, scientists, and mystics alike throughout the ages. It encompasses our subjective experience of the world, our sense of self-awareness, and our capacity for thought, perception, and emotion. Yet, despite centuries of inquiry, the nature of consciousness remains a deeply elusive and mysterious phenomenon.

At its core, consciousness embodies the essence of our inner world – the theater of the mind where thoughts, sensations, and perceptions converge to create our unique experience of reality. It is the awareness that illuminates our existence, granting us the capacity to reflect upon ourselves and the world around us. From the simplest of sensory experiences to the most profound states of contemplation, consciousness permeates every facet of our being, shaping our perceptions, desires, and actions.

Philosophers have long grappled with the question of what precisely constitutes consciousness and how it relates to the physical world. Some argue that consciousness is an emergent property of complex brain processes, arising from the intricate interactions of neurons and neural networks. According to this view, consciousness is reducible to the activity of the brain, and its mysteries can ultimately be unraveled through empirical investigation and scientific inquiry.

Others take a more holistic perspective, viewing consciousness as inseparable from the fabric of reality itself. From this vantage point, consciousness is not confined to the confines of the individual mind but is a fundamental aspect of the universe, pervading all of existence. This perspective is echoed in Eastern philosophies such as Advaita Vedanta and Buddhism, which emphasize the interconnectedness of all beings and the ultimate unity of consciousness.

Furthermore, consciousness raises profound questions about the nature of reality and the relationship between the observer and the observed. Quantum physics, for example, suggests that the act of observation plays a fundamental role in shaping the behavior of subatomic particles, blurring the distinction between the subjective and objective realms. This phenomenon underscores the intricate interplay between consciousness and the physical world, challenging conventional notions of causality and determinism.

Moreover, consciousness poses profound ethical and existential questions about the nature of identity, free will, and the meaning of life. As conscious beings, we grapple with our mortality, our place in the cosmos, and the ultimate purpose of our existence. These existential concerns lie at the heart of human experience, driving us to seek meaning, connection, and transcendence in a world imbued with mystery and uncertainty.

In conclusion, consciousness stands as a profound and enigmatic aspect of human existence, embodying the essence of our inner world and shaping our experience of reality in profound ways. While philosophers, scientists, and mystics continue to probe its mysteries, the nature of consciousness remains an enduring enigma – a testament to the boundless depths of human inquiry and the inexhaustible mysteries of the mind.

8

What is Beauty?

Beauty, a concept as ancient as humanity itself, transcends mere aesthetic appreciation to touch upon the deepest dimensions of human experience. It is a quality that captivates our senses, stirs our emotions, and resonates with the very essence of our being. Yet, despite its ubiquity in human discourse, the nature of beauty remains an enigmatic and multifaceted phenomenon, defying easy definition and categorization.

At its core, beauty embodies a harmonious synthesis of form, proportion, and meaning that elicits a profound sense of pleasure and admiration. From the majestic peaks of snow-capped mountains to the delicate intricacies of a blooming flower, beauty manifests in a myriad of forms, transcending cultural boundaries and historical epochs. It is a quality that imbues the world with wonder and awe, inviting us to contemplate the mysteries of existence and our place within the cosmos.

Philosophers throughout history have grappled with the question of what precisely constitutes beauty and how it is perceived and appreciated by individuals. For Plato, beauty was synonymous with the transcendent realm of the Forms, representing the highest ideals of truth, goodness, and symmetry. According to this view, beauty serves as a reflection of the divine order that permeates the universe, offering glimpses of the eternal and immutable amidst the flux of temporal existence.

In contrast, thinkers like Immanuel Kant emphasized the subjective nature of beauty, arguing that it resides in the eye of the beholder rather than in the object itself. According to Kant, beauty arises from the harmonious interplay of our cognitive faculties, eliciting a disinterested pleasure that transcends personal desire or utility. From this perspective, beauty is a product of human perception and interpretation, shaped by cultural, social, and psychological factors.

Moreover, beauty raises profound questions about the relationship between aesthetics and ethics, challenging us to consider the moral dimensions of our aesthetic judgments. Can beauty serve as a source of moral inspiration and upliftment, guiding us towards higher ideals of compassion, empathy, and justice? Or does the pursuit of beauty risk succumbing to superficiality, narcissism, and hedonism, leading us astray from the path of virtue and integrity?

Furthermore, beauty invites us to reflect upon the ephemeral nature of existence and the transient beauty of the world. Like a fleeting sunset or a fading melody, beauty is imbued with a sense of impermanence that lends it an added poignancy and depth. It is a reminder of the fragility of life and the inevitability of change, urging us to cherish each moment and savor the beauty that surrounds us before it fades into memory.

In conclusion, beauty is a multifaceted and elusive phenomenon that transcends the boundaries of language, culture, and time. It is a quality that resonates with the deepest dimensions of human experience, stirring our emotions, inspiring our creativity, and enriching our lives in myriad ways. While the nature of beauty may remain a mystery, its enduring presence in the world serves as a testament to the boundless depths of human perception and imagination.

9

Do we have free will?

The question of whether we possess free will is one of the oldest and most contentious issues in philosophy, stirring debates among thinkers from ancient times to the present day. At its essence, the inquiry into free will probes the nature of human agency and the extent to which individuals have the capacity to make choices that are truly independent of external influences.

On one hand, proponents of free will argue that humans possess the ability to deliberate, choose, and act in ways that are not wholly determined by prior causes or external factors. According to this view, our consciousness grants us the freedom to weigh options, consider consequences, and exercise control over our thoughts and actions. From the mundane decisions of everyday life to the most significant moral dilemmas, we experience a sense of autonomy that distinguishes us from mere automatons.

However, the concept of free will faces formidable challenges, particularly from the perspective of determinism – the notion that all events, including human actions, are ultimately determined by prior causes. According to determinism, every choice we make is the inevitable result of a complex web of causal factors, including genetics, upbringing, social conditioning, and environmental influences. From this standpoint, our apparent freedom of choice is illusory, as our decisions are merely the product of deterministic processes beyond our conscious control.

Moreover, modern neuroscience has raised further doubts about the existence of free will, suggesting that our brain activity precedes our conscious awareness of making a decision. Experiments measuring brain activity have shown that neural processes associated with decision-making occur before individuals report being aware of having made a choice. This has led some researchers to conclude that our sense of agency may be a post hoc illusion, with our brains merely rationalizing decisions that have already been predetermined at a subconscious level.

However, the debate over free will is far from settled, with scholars offering a range of perspectives that seek to reconcile the apparent tension between determinism and human agency. Some propose compatibilism, which contends that free will can coexist with determinism by redefining freedom as the ability to act in accordance with one's desires and motivations, even if those desires are ultimately shaped by external factors.

Others advocate for a more nuanced understanding of free will that acknowledges the role of indeterminacy and randomness in the universe. Quantum mechanics, for example, suggests that certain events at the subatomic level are inherently probabilistic, introducing an element of uncertainty into the deterministic framework. While this does not necessarily prove the existence of free will, it opens the door to the possibility of genuine spontaneity and choice within a universe governed by probabilistic laws.

In conclusion, the question of whether we possess free will remains a deeply complex and multifaceted issue, touching upon fundamental aspects of human consciousness, morality, and the nature of reality itself. While the determinist challenge poses significant obstacles to the concept of free will, proponents continue to defend the idea of human agency, emphasizing the experiential reality of choice and the importance of moral responsibility in human affairs. Whether free will ultimately exists as a metaphysical reality or a psychological illusion, the quest to understand our capacity for choice continues to be a central concern in philosophy and science alike.

10

The Meaning of Life and the Concept of Absurdism

The quest for the meaning of life has been a central theme in philosophy, literature, and religion for centuries. It is a profound and deeply personal question that touches on our very existence. Amidst various interpretations and theories, one particularly thought-provoking perspective is the concept of absurdism, prominently explored by the French philosopher and writer Albert Camus.

Understanding the Meaning of Life

At its core, the search for life's meaning is an exploration of purpose and value. Different philosophical traditions offer varied answers:

1. Religious Perspectives: Many religious beliefs propose that life's meaning is derived from a divine source. For instance, Christianity posits that living in accordance with God's will and achieving salvation is the ultimate purpose.

2. Existentialist Perspectives: Existentialists like Jean-Paul Sartre argue that life inherently has no meaning, and it is up to individuals to create their own purpose through actions and choices.

3. Humanist Perspectives: Humanism suggests that meaning is found in human relationships, achievements, and the pursuit of knowledge and happiness.

While these perspectives provide a range of answers, they all grapple with the fundamental question: Why do we exist?

Absurdism: Confronting the Chaos

Absurdism, particularly as articulated by Albert Camus, presents a unique approach to the question of life's meaning. Absurdism arises from the conflict between humans' natural desire to find inherent meaning in life and the silent, indifferent universe that offers no such answers.

The Absurd Hero: In his seminal work, *The Myth of Sisyphus*, Camus uses the Greek myth of Sisyphus to illustrate his concept of the absurd hero. Condemned to roll a boulder up a hill for eternity, only to have it roll back down each time, Sisyphus embodies the human struggle for meaning in a meaningless world. Despite the futility of his task, Camus imagines Sisyphus as happy, finding purpose in the struggle itself.

Living with the Absurd: According to Camus, recognizing the absurdity of existence can lead to a form of liberation. Rather than succumbing to despair, we can embrace the absurd and live fully in the present. This requires rejecting false hopes and embracing life's unpredictability and inherent lack of meaning.

The Three Responses to Absurdism

Camus identifies three potential responses to the absurd condition:

1. Suicide: Camus considers this the ultimate rejection of the absurd. By ending one's life, an individual seeks to escape the lack of meaning.

2. Philosophical Suicide: This involves embracing religious or metaphysical beliefs that provide comforting but ultimately unfounded answers to life's meaning.

3. Acceptance and Defiance: The most authentic response, according to Camus, is to accept the absurdity of existence and live with it. This means continuing to search for meaning, even knowing it may never be found.

Embracing the Absurd: Practical Implications

Living with an awareness of the absurd can profoundly affect how we approach life:

1. Authenticity: By accepting the absurd, individuals are encouraged to live authentically, making choices based on personal values rather than societal expectations.

2. Freedom: The realization that life has no predetermined

meaning can be liberating, offering a sense of freedom to create one's own purpose.

3. Presence: Absurdism emphasizes living in the moment, appreciating the beauty and experiences of life without being fixated on finding ultimate meaning.

4. Solidarity: Recognizing the shared human condition of confronting the absurd can foster a sense of solidarity and empathy among people.

The search for the meaning of life is a journey fraught with questions, doubts, and discoveries. Absurdism, with its stark acknowledgment of the conflict between our desire for meaning and the universe's indifference, offers a compelling framework. By embracing the absurd and finding purpose in the struggle itself, we can live more authentically and fully, savoring the transient and unpredictable nature of existence. In the words of Camus, we must imagine Sisyphus happy, for in the very act of pushing the boulder, he finds his meaning.

<h1 style="text-align:center">11</h1>

The concept of time: Is it real or an illusion?

The nature of time has been a subject of fascination and debate for philosophers, scientists, and theologians for millennia. Is time a fundamental part of the universe, or is it merely an illusion created by our consciousness? This question touches on deep aspects of reality, perception, and the human experience.

Time in Physics:

Newtonian Time: In classical physics, Isaac Newton viewed time as absolute and linear, flowing uniformly regardless of the events within the universe. According to Newton, time was a constant, a backdrop against which the drama of the cosmos unfolded.

Relativistic Time: Albert Einstein's theory of relativity revolutionized our understanding of time. In Einstein's universe, time is relative, intertwined with space to form the fabric of spacetime. Time can stretch and contract depending on the observer's speed and the gravitational field they are in. For instance, time passes slower near massive objects (a phenomenon known as time dilation). This suggests that time is not a universal constant but rather a variable, influenced by the conditions of the universe.

Philosophical Perspectives on Time:

Presentism vs. Eternalism: Philosophers debate whether only the present is real (presentism) or if the past, present, and future all coexist equally (eternalism). Presentists argue that only the current moment exists, and the past and future are mere abstractions. Eternalists, on the other hand, view time as a dimension similar to space, where all moments exist simultaneously, and our perception of "now" is just a point in this temporal landscape.

The Illusion of Time: Some philosophers and scientists argue that time might be an illusion. This view is partly inspired by the block universe theory, which suggests that time is a static dimension and that our perception of its flow is a cognitive construct. According to this theory, all events are fixed within a four-dimensional spacetime block, and our consciousness moves through this block, creating the illusion of time passing.

Time and Human Perception:

Psychological Time: Human experience of time is subjective and can vary widely. For instance, time seems to fly when we are engaged in enjoyable activities and crawl during periods of boredom or discomfort. This subjective experience of time indicates that our perception of its passage is influenced by cognitive and emotional states, suggesting that at least part of what we perceive as time is a construct of the mind.

Temporal Illusions: Research in cognitive psychology has identified various temporal illusions, such as the "oddball effect," where unusual events are perceived to last longer than ordinary ones. These illusions provide insights into how our brain processes time and support the idea that our perception of time is not a direct reflection of an external reality but a product of our mental processes.

Time in Metaphysics and Mysticism:

Time in Metaphysics: Many metaphysical theories explore time as a fundamental aspect of reality. Some propose that time is a fundamental dimension, similar to space, while others argue that it emerges from more basic physical processes. These theories often intersect with questions about causality, determinism, and the nature of existence.

Mystical and Eastern Philosophies: Various mystical and Eastern philosophical traditions offer alternative views on time. For example, in Buddhism, time is often seen as cyclical rather than linear, with existence undergoing endless cycles of birth, death, and rebirth (samsara). Similarly, some interpretations of Hindu philosophy view time as a series of cosmic cycles. These perspectives challenge the linear, Western conception of time and offer a more fluid, holistic view.

Implications of Time's Nature

Scientific Research and Technology: Our understanding of time has profound implications for scientific research and technology. For instance, time dilation must be accounted for in the precise timing systems of GPS satellites. Advances in quantum mechanics and theories of quantum gravity also hinge on a deeper understanding of time.

Philosophical and Existential Questions: The nature of time raises important philosophical and existential questions. If time is an illusion, what does that mean for our understanding of life, death, and the continuity of identity? If the past, present, and future coexist, how do we conceptualize free will and determinism?

The question of whether time is real or an illusion remains one of the most profound and challenging in both science and philosophy. While physics provides models that describe time as a flexible and relative dimension, philosophy and psychology reveal that our experience of time is deeply subjective and potentially illusory. As our understanding of the universe evolves, so too will our conception of time, continuing to intrigue and inspire thinkers across disciplines.

12

The Relationship Between Art and Emotion

Art has been an intrinsic part of human culture and expression for thousands of years, serving as a powerful medium to convey and evoke emotions. The relationship between art and emotion is complex and multifaceted, encompassing various forms of art and numerous psychological and philosophical perspectives.

Art as a Medium for Emotional Expression:

Historical Context: Historically, art has been a means for individuals and societies to express their emotions, beliefs, and values. From the cave paintings of prehistoric times to the digital art of today, humans have used visual, auditory, and performative arts to convey a wide range of emotions—from joy and love to sorrow and anger.

Artist's Emotions: The emotions of the artist often play a crucial role in the creation of art. Artists channel their feelings into their work, using it as a form of catharsis or communication. For instance, Vincent van Gogh's turbulent emotions are vividly depicted in his bold, expressive brushstrokes and vibrant colors, giving viewers insight into his inner world.

The Emotional Impact on the Audience:
Emotional Arousal: Art has a profound ability to evoke emotions in its audience. Music can induce a range of feelings from excitement to melancholy; visual art can inspire awe or contemplation; literature can elicit empathy or provoke thought. This emotional arousal is a key aspect of the aesthetic experience.

Empathy and Connection: Art allows viewers to connect with the emotions and experiences of others. Through a painting, a piece of music, or a novel, individuals can empathize with the artist's emotional state or the characters' experiences, fostering a sense of shared humanity.

Psychological and Neuroscientific Perspectives:
Affective Neuroscience: Neuroscientific research has begun to uncover the brain mechanisms underlying the emotional responses to art. Studies using neuroimaging techniques show that engaging with art activates brain regions involved in emotion processing, such as the amygdala and the orbitofrontal cortex.

Art Therapy: The therapeutic use of art highlights its powerful connection to emotion. Art therapy leverages the expressive nature of art to help individuals process and heal from emotional trauma, stress, and mental health disorders. Creating art can help patients express emotions they might find difficult to verbalize, providing a non-verbal outlet for their feelings.

Philosophical Perspectives on Art and Emotion:

Aesthetic Theories: Various aesthetic theories explore the relationship between art and emotion. The theory of expressionism, for example, posits that art is fundamentally an expression of emotion. In contrast, formalism emphasizes the importance of the formal qualities of art, such as composition and technique, rather than its emotional content.

Catharsis: The concept of catharsis, originating from Aristotle's *Poetics*, suggests that engaging with art can provide an emotional release for the audience. By experiencing emotions through art, individuals can achieve a sense of purification and emotional renewal.

Tolstoy's View: Leo Tolstoy, in his work *What Is Art?*, argued that the purpose of art is to communicate the artist's emotions to the audience, creating a shared emotional experience. He believed that the best art connects people by conveying the artist's sincere and deeply felt emotions.

Forms of Art and Their Emotional Impact

Visual Arts: Paintings, sculptures, and other visual arts use color, form, and composition to evoke emotions. The emotional impact can be immediate and visceral, as seen in Edvard Munch's *The Scream*, which powerfully conveys a sense of existential angst.

Music: Music is perhaps the most direct form of art in terms of emotional impact. Melodies, harmonies, and rhythms can evoke a wide range of emotions without the need for words. Beethoven's symphonies, for instance, can convey intense passion and profound sorrow.

Literature: Literature uses language to explore and evoke emotions. Through character development, narrative structure, and stylistic choices, authors can create deep emotional resonance. The works of Fyodor Dostoevsky, for example, delve into complex emotional and psychological landscapes.

Performing Arts: Theatre, dance, and film combine visual, auditory, and performative elements to create rich emotional experiences. The immediacy and dynamism of live performance can make the emotional impact particularly powerful, as seen in the tragic plays of William Shakespeare or the expressive choreography of Martha Graham.

The relationship between art and emotion is a dynamic interplay that enhances both the creation and appreciation of art. Artists use their work to express and communicate emotions, while audiences engage with art to experience and process their own feelings. This profound connection underscores the importance of art in human life, serving as a bridge between the internal emotional world and the external expression of those emotions. Through this interplay, art continues to enrich our understanding of ourselves and others, fostering empathy, connection, and emotional depth.

13

Consciousness and Its Origins

Consciousness is one of the most profound and elusive phenomena in the universe, lying at the intersection of philosophy, neuroscience, psychology, and even quantum physics. Understanding consciousness—what it is, how it arises, and what its origins are—remains one of the greatest challenges in both science and philosophy.

Defining Consciousness:

Consciousness refers to the state of being aware of and able to think about oneself, one's surroundings, and one's thoughts and feelings. It encompasses a range of experiences, including sensory perceptions, thoughts, emotions, and the sense of self.

Phenomenal Consciousness: This aspect refers to the subjective experience or the "what it is like" to be conscious. It is the qualitative, first-person perspective of experiencing the world.

Access Consciousness: This involves the ability to report on mental states and use them in reasoning and guiding behavior. It is the functional aspect of consciousness that allows for cognitive processing and action.

Philosophical Perspectives:

Dualism: Proposed by René Descartes, dualism posits that the mind and body are separate entities. According to dualism, consciousness is a non-physical substance that interacts with the physical body.

Materialism: Materialists argue that consciousness arises from physical processes within the brain. This perspective views mental states as brain states, governed by neurobiological processes.

Panpsychism: This theory suggests that consciousness is a fundamental aspect of all matter, with even the smallest particles having some form of proto-consciousness. According to panpsychism, complex consciousness emerges from the combination of these basic units.

Idealism: Idealists, such as George Berkeley, argue that reality is fundamentally mental and that material objects exist only insofar as they are perceived by a conscious mind.

Scientific Approaches to Consciousness:

Neuroscience: Modern neuroscience seeks to understand consciousness by studying the brain's structure and function. Techniques such as functional magnetic resonance imaging (fMRI) and electroencephalography (EEG) have revealed correlations between brain activity and conscious experiences.

- **Global Workspace Theory**: Proposed by Bernard Baars, this theory suggests that consciousness arises from the integration of information in a global workspace within the brain. This workspace allows for the sharing and broadcasting of information across different neural networks.

- **Integrated Information Theory (IIT)**: Developed by Giulio Tononi, IIT posits that consciousness is a result of integrated information. According to this theory, the more interconnected and integrated the neural network, the higher the level of consciousness.

Evolutionary Biology: From an evolutionary perspective, consciousness is seen as an adaptation that has provided survival advantages. The ability to be aware, reflect, and make complex decisions would have been beneficial for early humans in navigating their environment, social interactions, and threats.

The Hard Problem of Consciousness:

The "hard problem," a term coined by philosopher David Chalmers, refers to the difficulty of explaining why and how subjective experiences (qualia) arise from physical processes in the brain. While neuroscience can describe the mechanisms of brain function, it struggles to explain why these processes result in conscious experience.

Theories on the Origins of Consciousness

Emergent Properties: One theory is that consciousness emerges from complex interactions among neurons. Just as wetness emerges from the interaction of water molecules, consciousness might emerge from neural activity.

Quantum Theories: Some theories, such as those proposed by Roger Penrose and Stuart Hameroff, suggest that consciousness may arise from quantum processes within brain microtubules. These theories are controversial and remain speculative but offer an intriguing perspective on the origins of consciousness.

Primordial Consciousness: Another hypothesis is that consciousness has always existed as a fundamental aspect of the universe. This aligns with panpsychism and suggests that consciousness did not emerge but is an intrinsic part of reality.

Challenges and Future Directions:

Interdisciplinary Research: Understanding consciousness requires a multidisciplinary approach, integrating insights from neuroscience, psychology, philosophy, and artificial intelligence.

Artificial Intelligence and Consciousness: As AI systems become more sophisticated, questions arise about the potential for artificial consciousness. Can machines be conscious, or is consciousness uniquely tied to biological processes?

Ethical Implications: Advances in understanding and potentially manipulating consciousness have profound ethical implications, affecting fields such as medicine, artificial intelligence, and even legal definitions of personhood.

Consciousness remains one of the greatest mysteries of science and philosophy. Its origins and nature are subjects of ongoing debate and research. While significant strides have been made in understanding the neural correlates of consciousness, the subjective experience of being conscious and the fundamental nature of consciousness continue to challenge and inspire thinkers across disciplines. The quest to unravel the enigma of consciousness not only advances our scientific knowledge but also deepens our understanding of what it means to be human.

14

The Role of Existential Anxiety and Despair

Existential anxiety and despair are central themes in existential philosophy, profoundly influencing our understanding of human existence. These concepts explore the deep-seated feelings of unease, uncertainty, and meaninglessness that arise from the human condition. Existential thinkers such as Søren Kierkegaard, Friedrich Nietzsche, Jean-Paul Sartre, and Martin Heidegger have extensively examined these emotions, offering insights into their origins, implications, and potential resolutions.

Understanding Existential Anxiety:

Definition: Existential anxiety, or existential angst, refers to a pervasive sense of dread and unease that stems from the realization of life's inherent uncertainties, the inevitability of death, and the responsibility of shaping one's own existence.

Kierkegaard's Perspective: Søren Kierkegaard, often considered the father of existentialism, described anxiety as a fundamental aspect of the human condition. In *The Concept of*

Anxiety, he posits that anxiety arises from the freedom to make choices and the accompanying responsibility. This freedom is both exhilarating and terrifying, as it forces individuals to confront the potential consequences of their actions.

Heidegger's View: Martin Heidegger explored existential anxiety in *Being and Time*. He argued that anxiety reveals the "nothingness" of existence, stripping away the superficial layers of everyday life and exposing the individual to the reality of their finite being. This encounter with nothingness compels individuals to confront their own mortality and the meaning of their existence.

The Nature of Existential Despair:

Definition: Existential despair is a profound feeling of hopelessness and meaninglessness. It occurs when individuals fail to find purpose or significance in their lives, leading to a sense of existential crisis.

Sartre's Concept of "Bad Faith": Jean-Paul Sartre described existential despair in terms of "bad faith," a condition where individuals deceive themselves to avoid confronting the truth of their freedom and responsibility. By living inauthentically and conforming to societal expectations, individuals escape the anxiety of choice but ultimately experience despair due to the lack of genuine purpose.

Kierkegaard's Stages of Despair: Kierkegaard outlined different stages of despair in *The Sickness Unto Death*. He believed that despair results from a misalignment between one's finite self (the individual) and the infinite self (the ideal or divine). This misalignment can manifest in various forms, such as the despair of not being aware of having a self, the despair of not willing to be oneself, and the despair of willing to be oneself without acknowledging the transcendent.

The Role and Impact of Existential Anxiety and Despair:

Catalysts for Authentic Living: Existential anxiety and despair can act as catalysts for living authentically. By confronting these emotions, individuals are compelled to reflect on their values, beliefs, and choices. This self-examination can lead to a more authentic and meaningful existence, as individuals align their actions with their true selves.

Motivation for Change: These existential feelings can motivate individuals to make significant changes in their lives. The discomfort of anxiety and despair can drive people to seek new paths, explore different possibilities, and strive for personal growth and fulfillment.

Understanding Human Existence: Existential anxiety and despair offer profound insights into the human condition. They reveal the inherent uncertainties and challenges of existence, emphasizing the importance of individual responsibility and the quest for meaning in a seemingly indifferent universe.

Creativity and Expression: Many artists, writers, and thinkers have channeled their existential anxiety and despair into creative expression. The exploration of these emotions in art and literature can provide catharsis for both creators and audiences, fostering a deeper understanding of the human experience.

Resolving Existential Anxiety and Despair:

Embracing Freedom and Responsibility: Acknowledging and embracing one's freedom and the associated responsibility can mitigate existential anxiety. By accepting the power to shape their own lives, individuals can find empowerment and purpose.

Living Authentically: Authenticity involves living in accordance with one's true self, rather than conforming to external expectations. This requires continuous self-reflection, honesty, and the courage to make choices that reflect one's genuine values and desires.

Finding Meaning: Viktor Frankl, in his seminal work *Man's Search for Meaning*, emphasized the importance of finding meaning in life, even in the face of suffering. According to Frankl, meaning can be derived from various sources, such as relationships, work, and personal growth. By identifying and pursuing meaningful goals, individuals can transcend existential despair.

Acceptance and Commitment: Existential therapists often encourage acceptance of life's uncertainties and limitations. By committing to actions that align with one's values, individuals can navigate existential anxiety and despair with resilience and purpose.

Existential anxiety and despair are intrinsic aspects of the human experience, reflecting our deep awareness of freedom, mortality, and the quest for meaning. While these emotions can be challenging, they also offer valuable opportunities for growth, self-discovery, and authentic living. By embracing our existential condition and seeking meaningful paths, we can transform anxiety and despair into catalysts for a richer, more fulfilling existence.

15

The Nature of Beauty and Artistic Value

The nature of beauty and artistic value has long been a subject of philosophical inquiry and debate. These concepts delve into the essence of aesthetics, exploring why certain forms, colors, sounds, and ideas are considered beautiful and how we ascribe value to artistic creations. The exploration of beauty and artistic value intersects with various disciplines, including philosophy, psychology, art history, and cultural studies.

Defining Beauty:

Subjective vs. Objective Beauty: One of the central debates in aesthetics is whether beauty is subjective (based on individual perception) or objective (inherent in the object itself).

- **Subjective Beauty**: From this perspective, beauty is in the eye of the beholder. What one person finds beautiful, another may not. This view emphasizes personal, cultural, and contextual differences in aesthetic appreciation.
- **Objective Beauty**: This view posits that beauty has inher-

ent qualities that can be universally recognized, regardless of individual differences. Philosophers like Plato and Immanuel Kant have argued for certain objective standards of beauty, such as harmony, proportion, and symmetry.

Theories of Beauty: Various theories have been proposed to explain the nature of beauty.

- **Platonism**: Plato viewed beauty as a reflection of a higher, ideal form. According to this view, physical manifestations of beauty are imperfect copies of this ideal.
- **Kantian Aesthetics**: Immanuel Kant argued that beauty is a result of a harmonious relationship between the faculties of understanding and imagination. He introduced the concept of "disinterested pleasure," suggesting that true aesthetic appreciation is free from personal desire or practical considerations.
- **Evolutionary Aesthetics**: Some theories propose that our sense of beauty has evolutionary roots, linked to reproductive success and survival. For instance, symmetrical features might be perceived as beautiful because they signal health and genetic fitness.

Artistic Value

Intrinsic vs. Extrinsic Value: Artistic value can be intrinsic (value found within the artwork itself) or extrinsic (value derived from external factors).

- **Intrinsic Value**: This refers to the inherent qualities of an artwork, such as its composition, technique, and emotional impact. An artwork is valuable for its own sake, appreciated for its beauty, craftsmanship, or expressive power.

- **Extrinsic Value**: This encompasses factors outside the artwork itself, such as historical significance, cultural context, market value, and the reputation of the artist. These factors can influence how an artwork is perceived and valued.

Philosophical Perspectives on Artistic Value: Different philosophical approaches offer various insights into the nature of artistic value.

- **Formalism**: This approach emphasizes the formal qualities of an artwork, such as line, color, shape, and composition. Formalists argue that these elements are the primary sources of artistic value, independent of context or content.
- **Expressionism**: Expressionists focus on the emotional and expressive power of art. Artistic value lies in the ability of an artwork to convey emotions and provoke a deep response in the viewer.
- **Institutional Theory**: This theory, articulated by George Dickie, suggests that an artwork's value is determined by its recognition and acceptance within the art world. The value is conferred by institutions such as museums, galleries, and critics.

The Interplay Between Beauty and Artistic Value:

Beauty as a Component of Artistic Value: Beauty often contributes to the artistic value of a work, but it is not the sole determinant. An artwork can be highly valued for its historical importance, innovative technique, or emotional depth, even if it does not conform to traditional standards of beauty.

Challenging Conventional Beauty: Many modern and contemporary artists challenge conventional notions of beauty, exploring themes of discomfort, ugliness, and the sublime. These works push the boundaries of aesthetic appreciation and highlight the complex nature of artistic value.

Cultural and Temporal Variability: Concepts of beauty and artistic value are not static; they vary across cultures and time periods. What is considered beautiful or valuable in one culture or era might not be in another. This variability underscores the importance of context in understanding aesthetics.

The Role of the Viewer:

Active Engagement: The viewer plays a crucial role in the appreciation of beauty and artistic value. Active engagement, interpretation, and emotional response contribute to the overall experience of an artwork.

Personal and Collective Experience: Aesthetic appreciation can be both a personal and collective experience. Personal taste and individual experiences influence how one perceives beauty and artistic value, while collective cultural norms and shared histories shape communal aesthetic judgments.

The nature of beauty and artistic value is a rich and multifaceted area of inquiry that bridges subjective experience and objective qualities, intrinsic merits, and extrinsic factors. By exploring these concepts, we gain deeper insights into the human condition, our cultural heritage, and the ways we express and perceive the world. Whether through the lens of philosophy, art history, or psychology, the study of beauty and artistic value continues to inspire and challenge our understanding of aesthetics.

<h1 style="text-align:center">16</h1>

The Role of Intentionality in Shaping Experience

Intentionality is a core concept in philosophy and psychology, referring to the capacity of the mind to be directed towards objects, events, or states of affairs. It is the quality of mental states that involves an awareness of something or about something. This concept plays a crucial role in understanding how our experiences are shaped, as it underscores the active and directed nature of human consciousness.

Understanding Intentionality:

Philosophical Origins: The concept of intentionality was extensively developed by the philosopher Franz Brentano in the 19th century. Brentano distinguished between mental phenomena, which are characterized by intentionality, and physical phenomena, which are not. He argued that every mental act is directed towards an object—whether real or imagined.

Husserl's Phenomenology: Edmund Husserl, a student of Brentano, further elaborated on intentionality in his phenomenological philosophy. Husserl emphasized that consciousness is always consciousness of something, meaning that our mental states are always about an object or situation. He introduced the idea of "intentional acts" and "intentional objects" to describe the relationship between the mind and the world.

Intentionality and Experience:

Directedness of Consciousness: Intentionality is fundamental to how we experience the world. It is through intentionality that we perceive, think about, and engage with our environment. For example, when we see a tree, our consciousness is directed towards the tree, and our perception is structured by this intentional act.

Meaning and Context: Intentionality also involves the meaning and context of experiences. The way we interpret and understand our experiences is shaped by our intentions. When we read a book, our understanding and interpretation of the text are influenced by our intention to grasp the meaning, comprehend the plot, and engage with the characters.

Subjectivity and Objectivity: Intentionality bridges the subjective and objective aspects of experience. While our experiences are subjective, they are directed towards objects that we perceive as existing independently of our minds. This dual aspect of intentionality highlights the interplay between our internal mental states and the external world.

The Role of Intentionality in Perception:

Perceptual Experience: In perception, intentionality shapes the way we organize and make sense of sensory information. Our perceptual experience is not a passive reception of stimuli but an active process of interpreting and understanding what we perceive. For instance, when looking at a complex painting, our attention and intentionality guide us to focus on specific elements, shapes, and colors, forming a coherent interpretation of the artwork.

Gestalt Psychology: Gestalt psychology emphasizes that our perception is organized by innate principles that guide how we group and interpret sensory information. These principles reflect the intentional structure of our perceptual experience, as we actively seek to create meaningful wholes from the parts we perceive.

Intentionality in Thought and Imagination:

Directed Thought: Our thoughts are intentional in that they are always about something. When we think about a problem, plan for the future, or reflect on past experiences, our thoughts are directed towards specific objects, ideas, or scenarios. This directedness helps structure our cognitive processes and enables us to navigate complex mental tasks.

Imagination and Creativity: Intentionality also plays a key role in imagination and creativity. When we imagine something, we are intentionally directing our minds towards a mental representation that is not currently present in our immediate environment. This intentional act allows us to create new ideas, envision possibilities, and engage in creative thinking.

Intentionality and Emotions:

Emotionally Charged Intentional States: Emotions are inherently intentional—they are directed towards particular objects or situations. For example, when we feel anger, it is typically directed towards someone or something that we perceive as having wronged us. Our emotional experiences are shaped by our intentional stance towards the objects of our emotions.

Affective Intentionality: The intentionality of emotions involves both the cognitive appraisal of a situation and the affective response to it. This dual aspect means that our emotions are influenced by how we interpret and understand the situations we encounter, highlighting the interplay between cognitive and emotional intentionality.

Intentionality in Action

Purposeful Action: Our actions are guided by intentionality. When we perform an action, we do so with a certain intention or goal in mind. This intentionality shapes how we plan, execute, and evaluate our actions. For instance, when cooking a meal, our actions are directed towards the goal of preparing a specific dish, and each step is guided by this intention.

Agency and Autonomy: Intentionality is central to our sense of agency and autonomy. By directing our actions with purpose and intention, we exercise control over our behavior and make deliberate choices. This intentional control is fundamental to our experience of being autonomous agents capable of shaping our own lives.

Intentionality is a foundational concept that profoundly influences our experiences, perceptions, thoughts, emotions, and actions. It highlights the active and directed nature of human consciousness, emphasizing that our mental states are always about something. By understanding the role of intentionality, we gain deeper insights into how we engage with the world, interpret our experiences, and exercise our agency.

This understanding enriches our appreciation of the complexity and richness of human consciousness and its capacity to shape our lived experience.